Wellness Journal
Fresno, CA 93720

Copyright 2022 by Sensational Tiger Productions

All rights reserved.

Erin Garcia, Christian Bajusz, and Ashlyn Garrett

sensationalstims.com

Table of Contents

Property of Page 1

Who Is This For? 2

Why This Wellness Journal? 3

Stimming Explained 4-5

(Re)Discovering Our Senses 6-9

Example Entry 10

Affirmations Explained 11

Feelings Defined 12-13

Important Vocabulary 14-17

Coloring Pages 19-25

Doodle Pages 26-31

Journal Entries 32-85

Extra Notes 86-95

Year In Review 96-97

About The Authors 98

Who Is This For?

It's for anyone who wants to grow psychologically. As a neurodivergent (ND) person, it is especially helpful. ND is the neurotype of people who aren't neurotypical. This term is often used for autistic people, but can also be used for others who aren't autistic, but still neurodivergent, like those with ADHD, OCD, Tourette's, etc. ND refers to unique variation in the way the brain processes information compared to neurotypical processing.

The Sensational Journal was designed especially for neurodivergent people. It is a companion that can be used to record daily experiences and emotions, discover patterns, and utilize the benefits of journaling.

Journaling helps people to find patterns in their experiences and emotions. It strengthens one's mindset through reflection, improves health and wellness, and enhances life.

If you are neurodivergent and haven't yet learned how to journal, this is the perfect tool for you. Many neurodivergent people have used these pages to help them gain insight into their thoughts, feelings, and experiences. And we hope you will use it, too!

Other helpful pages:

Stimming Explained (pg 4): When we understand why we stim, we understand ourselves. The stimming section addresses our sensory needs.

(Re)discovering Your Sensory Profile (pg 6-9): explains a variety of senses besides the commonly known five senses. There are many senses like proprioceptive, vestibular, and interoception that affect our lives tremendously. Understanding your senses is very important to your health and happiness and that's why this journal is "sensational" (get it?!).

Feelings and Affirmations (pg 11-13): lists and explains a variety of feelings for journalers to help identify their feelings. The more you can identify your feelings, the easier it gets to understand them.

Coloring pages (pg 19-25): These coloring pages are scattered throughout the journal. They are just plain fun! Color whenever you feel like it!(Or don't, if coloring isn't your thing!) There is no wrong way to do this journal!

Doodling pages (pg 26-31): Doodling is fun and a great way to relax. Sometimes it helps your mind focus.

Year in Review (pg 94-95): a page where time should be taken to reflect on your journey at the end of the year.

Why This Wellness Journal?

Weekly journal entries help people:
- ☑ Gain self-confidence
- ☑ Improve communication skills
- ☑ Achieve goals
- ☑ Encourage you during tough times
- ☑ Promote gratitude and overall wellness
- ☑ Help you (re)discover your brilliance
- ☑ Remind you that you are sensational!

Where and When Should I Use This?

Dedicate one day a week to journal.

Find a quiet, comfortable place to write and reflect for 10-15 minutes.

Journals can be done alone or with help.

Thank You!

We hope this journal inspires you to create your own story and helps you find your inner strength, brilliance, and joy.

Start your Sensational Journal today! You'll be so proud you did.

Sincerely,
The Sensational Stims Team
@sensationalstims
Sensationalstims.com

Why is there a "stimming section" in my journal entries? I've never heard of stimming!

This journal has a special section to address our senses and sensory needs.
That's why this journal is "sensational" (get it?!).
Senses are things we feel on the inside but are difficult to see from the outside.

Things that happen on the inside of the body can be difficult to understand. Because we cannot see them happening, they might be hard to explain. But stims are our clues for those inside (a.k.a. internal) experiences!

Stimming is how our bodies move when we are having an internal experience.

That's why we have the magnifying glass in the book and on the first page of this journal. A scientist or a detective might use a magnifying glass to look very closely at clues to understand what is happening. Just like them, you can better understand your internal experience by looking closely at your stims.

Most people stim, even though some people do not even know why they're doing it. For some, stimming is very important. We never want to stop someone from stimming, unless it's harmful.

Knowing why we stim matters a lot.

People stim for a variety of reasons. Stimming mainly helps people manage their emotions. Just like the book The Case of Sensational Stims, this journal helps us better understand ourselves and others, without judgment.

Sometimes people stim because of feelings they have, and other times it's because of something happening in the environment. For example, some stim because they're happy, or sad, or anxious, or excited, or angry. Otherse stim because it's too hot or too cold, or too loud, or too bright, or they're just really hungry. Sometimes the reasons and ways people stim change.

We all have different reasons for stimming because we are all different. Most people stim.

When you can know the answers to these questions, you can better understand your feelings and your body's needs! Like a detective, you'll want to uncover why you're stimming. There's a place in your entry to note if you've stimmed a lot during the week. If you have been, it's a hint you might be working through a difficult challenge, or may need extra support.

When we understand why we stim, we understand ourselves. Understanding stimming allows us to understand and honor our needs and feelings. If you want to read more about stimming, check out The Case of Sensational Stims on Amazon today in English or Spanish or follow @sensationalstims on Instagram or Facebook!

If you are stimming a lot because you're very overwhelmed but you cannot remove the reason for your stims, here are some ways to help calm yourself:

Some Ways We Stim

Please note this list doesn't include all types of stims. Can you think of any other stims? Do you do some of these stims when you feel happy? Sad? Anxious? What usually happens before you stim? How do you feel after?

- ☐ Singing/chanting/humming/making noises
- ☐ Repeatedly touching a texture we love (soft/squishy/etc.)
- ☐ Repeating a phrase/word over and over (echolalia)
- ☐ Rocking
- ☐ Jumping
- ☐ Chewing on something
- ☐ Pacing
- ☐ Shaking
- ☐ Dancing
- ☐ Flapping hands
- ☐ Biting your fingernails
- ☐ Twirling your hair around your fingers
- ☐ Cracking your knuckles or other joints
- ☐ Drumming fingers.
- ☐ Tapping your pencil
- ☐ Jiggling your foot
- ☐ Whistling

If you are stimming a lot because you're very overwhelmed but you cannot remove the reason for your stims, the next page has some ways to help you calm yourself:

Coping Effecively

Sit down
Rest

Connect
Focus on your senses and try to name things you can smell, taste, see, touch, and/or hear.

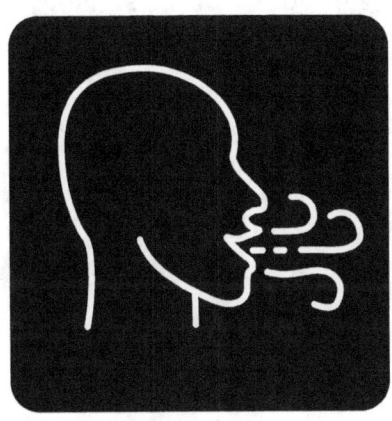

Breathe
Put one hand over your heart and one hand over your belly.

Count
Going backwards or forwards in multiples is a way to refocus your mind.

Remember
You're not in an emergency and slowing down is ok!

Honor
Acknowledge how you are feeling and that you are an amazing person!

(Re)Discovering Our Senses

Directions: This activity is designed to gain a basic understanding of a certain part of yourself that you may not know much about. This list is not exhaustive nor a medical diagnosis of any kind.

On a scale of 1-10 rate how important that sense is to you.

A score of 10 indicates this sense is extremely important to your health and wellness. A high score means this sense affects you very deeply; your life would be changed in a major way if that sense is affected. A score of 1 means it's minimally important and it is of no significant consequence. You may be unaware or unbothered by this sense. Even if you recognize it's important, this sense is not impacting you often. As time goes on, your ranking might change.

The point of this activity is to enhance your understanding of your unique sensory profile. This may help you understand some of the reasons for stimming.

If you know and understand your general sensory profile, making accommodations for yourself may be easier. Appropriate accommodations will promote your personal success and well-being.

Some of these senses may surprise you. Also, it could take a moment or two to uncover your sensory profile and needs. That's ok if it takes time. Take all the time you need!

Some of these senses are discussed in the book The Element: How Finding Your Passion Changes Everything by Ken Robinson and Lou Aronica. They write, "all of our senses contribute to our feelings of being in the world and our ability to function in it [...] (T)hey illustrate how profoundly our senses, however many we have and however they work, actually affect our understanding of the world and of ourselves. Yet many of us don't know or have even thought about them" (33).

Please note these ratings aren't to assess how smart or skilled you are at anything. Neither is rating something "high" or "low" an indicator of any one person's intelligence or worth. We also never want to try to "desensitize" ourselves, especially if we are very sensitive in one area. The point here is to understand our senses and ourselves better, and therefore give ourselves the accommodations and compassion we need.

Sense	Rating /10
Auditory Processing - the ability to interpret sounds. In central auditory processing, the brain must identify incoming sounds and then make an analysis of those sounds, THEN it attaches meaning to them. If you need to hear information in order to make sense of it, your auditory processing is really important. If regular sounds or loud noises hurt your ears and/or prevent you from hearing important information, and you're an auditory learner, this sense should be rated high. Or perhaps the pitch/tone of sounds is important for you and it bothers you deeply if the pitch/tone is off, you would rate auditory processing a 9/10 or a 10/10. A helpful accommodation for sensitive people is noise-canceling headphones or ear plugs.	/10
Visual Processing - the brain's ability to use and interpret visual information from the world around us. If you must "see" to understand something, this should be rated high. Maybe visual processing is not as important for you to understand important information, but you still feel that visual input is important, you might rank it a 5/10 or 6/10.	/10
Olfactory Processing - the special sense through which smells are perceived. The sense of smell has many functions, including detecting desirable foods, hazards, and pheromones, and plays a role in taste. If particular smells can put you in a good or bad mood, or if the smell of your area is important, you would rank this high. If you've never once considered smell in your daily living, rank it low. If you're very sensitive, be sure to pack essential oils to smell or a bandana/mask to cover your nose when needed.	/10
Oral Sensory Processing -how we process tactile input in our mouths. Oral sensory processing also contributes to the way we move our mouths, control our saliva, and produce sounds for clear speech. If eating particular foods bother you tremendously or bring you immense pleasure, this might receive a high ranking for you. Conversely, if eating is just something you do to survive and you barely taste anything, this would receive a low score. If oral sensory processing is important for you, you might always want to have gum on hand, or a chewy necklace to keep yourself calm and relaxed.	/10

Sense	Rating /10
Tactile Processing- the sensation of touch all over our skin. Some areas of our skin have more tactile receptors than other areas (e.g. mouth and hands). If touch is very important for you, you may want to be sure to always wear comfortable clothing that will not irritate your tactile skin. The tactile senses are important for identifying touch, pressure, pain, temperature and texture. Some more specific tactile senses are listed below, since these specific areas affect people a great deal. If the way clothing feels on your skin matters a lot and affects your mood and overall wellness, give it a high mark. If the texture of clothing has never bothered you at all, give it a low score.	/10
Thermoception- the sensation and perception of temperature, or more accurately, temperature differences from heat changes. Those who are seriously affected by heat or cold would give this a higher score than an individual who can wear shorts in a snowstorm, or are unaffected/unbothered by very warm temperatures. Remember this is not about your preference for a temperature, this is about how you sense temperature in your body.	/10
Nociception - sense of pain signaling and processing. Noxious stimulation is communicated through the peripheral and central nervous system. Nociceptors are specific receptors within the skin, muscle, skeletal structures, and viscera that detect potentially damaging stimuli. If you identify as very sensitive in this area, you might rank this very high. If you've ever been hurt, but weren't aware that you were hurt, you might rank this low. But please make sure you are safe; take time to take a daily inventory of yourself and your needs, especially if you don't have a strong nociception sense, take care to observe yourself and your surroundings to make sure you do not burn out.	/10
Equilibrioception- aka vestibular sense. The sense of balance and acceleration. A very skilled athlete or coordinated person might rank this one a 10. A person might also rank this one high if your balance significantly impacts your daily living in a negative way. Exercises that work on balance and practicing mindfulness can improve one's proprioception, as well as occupational therapy.	/10
Proprioception- Kinesthetic sense which gives us our understanding of where our limbs and the rest of our body are in space and relationship to each other. A person who identifies as "clumsy" might give themselves a low score on this sense. Someone who identifies as very coordinated and easily performs physical tasks might give themselves a high ranking.	/10

Sense	Rating /10
Intuition- the sense of "feeling" a truth or something that is likely without consciously learning it. An instinctive feeling. If you are in constant understanding of your "gut" feeling, this should be high. If you often use this sense to make decisions this would receive a high score. If you frequently struggle to "trust your gut" and it impacts you often, give this a high score. If this sense rarely impacts your life, give it a low score. If you have a low score on this one, taking time to ponder your thoughts and feelings can possibly help improve this sense, if you want to.	/10
Interoception-the sense that helps you understand and feel what's going on inside your body. People who struggle with the interoceptive sense may have trouble knowing when they feel hungry/full/hot/cold/ and/or thirsty. Having trouble with this sense can also make self-regulation a challenge. If self-regulation is difficult, you may find yourself melting down or shutting down unexpectedly. On this one, if you rarely recognize when you feel hungry/tired/hot/cold/etc., and it significantly impacts your life, you might want to rank this high. But if it doesn't impact your daily living often, you would rank it low. If you frequently have a sense of how you are feeling, and it impacts you deeply, give yourself a high ranking. Remember, there are no wrong answers, this is just a way to understand ourselves in a different way.	/10

Things to think or talk about after the activity:

Did you learn anything about your sensory profile?

Does having a name for the variety of senses offer any insights you may not have had before?

Sensory regulation is when people can regulate their senses by first being aware of them and their senses and then accommodating themselves in a way that suits their needs. Regulated people often have less anxiety, have more confidence and success. Regulating your senses can be difficult if you don't know what you need or what is vital for your body to thrive.

Sensory awareness leads to the ability for people to consciously manage their bodies so they feel safe and cared for. How might knowing about this help you or others in the future?

Example Entry:

Week of:
02/17/2022

My positive affirmation for this week is:
(Affirmations are simple, positive statements that everyone can do to frame their mindset. See the next page for definition and help)

I love learning and growing.

As I write this, I am feeling: #__1__
(see page 5-6 for feeling words- list what number your feeling falls under. This can help you when you reflect on the feelings you've had over the past few weeks. Any trends? Can you think about why?)

thrilled

I feel this way because/If I could compare my feelings to something it would be like...

I am thrilled like I just won the lottery when my cousin spent the night. We had fun!

A challenging thing/updates from last week:
(challenges are situations that may have caused you stress. List it here)

When I had to get a shot at the doctor's office. I was disappointed and frustrated. I know it had to be done and my dad held my hand.

The results from the test came back! My numbers look better than before!

I am grateful for/I want to remember:
(The practice of gratitude can change everything in a person's life. Making time to record moments of thankfulness has a powerful impact on your quality of life. Often, gratitude can be an inspirational thing, large or small. What did you notice?)

1. chocolate. For obvious reasons.
2. I watched some baby chicks hatch from their eggs at my friend's house! They had to work so hard to get out of their egg!

Have I stimmed lately?
  Yes
  No

How have I been stimming?

What does my stimming tell me?

Upcoming this week!
(This is to note important upcoming events. They can be related to school, sports, doctors appointments, tv shows- whatever you have coming up!)

Doctor appointment Tues- leave school at 11!
History test Thursday
Write Grandma a thank you note for this journal.
Gymnastics on Fri at 3

Purpose of Affirmations

Affirmations are simple, positive statements that everyone can do. They help set a person's frame of mind and are especially useful during challenging times. Affirmations are one way to create a growth mindset. This term was coined by psychologist Carol Dweck. She writes in her book <u>Mindset: The New Psychology of Success</u>, "In a growth mindset, people believe that their most basic abilities can be developed through dedication and hard work—brains and talent are just the starting point. This view creates a love of learning and a resilience that is essential for great accomplishment."

Please know that a growth mindset does not mean that everything is always perfect or you need to be falsely positive. In a growth mindset, people embrace the idea that each opportunity is a chance to deepen one's understanding and develop through experience. This journal will cultivate a growth mindset.

Determine your weekly affirmations by what you would like to have most in your life. Below are some examples of affirmations to use by topic. Use these or create your own!

Happiness: Today I choose to find joy in everything, big or small; life is meant to be savored.

Peace: I am calm and at peace.

Success: I have the power to create all the success I desire.

Wellness: I appreciate and love my body. Every action I take is a step towards my health and well-being.

Feelings Defined

Naming your feelings is important. Use this page to help name your feelings accurately. Feelings are neither right or wrong and they never last forever. In fact, you might feel more than one feeling at a time. Name whatever you feel, and feel free to update if you need!

#1. Happy
accepted- believed, welcomed
amazed- perplexed, stunned, in wonder
content-untroubled, at peace
curious- interested, full of questions
empowered- full of ability
excited- enthusiastic, eager
peaceful-relaxed, calm
playful- joyful, high-spirited
sensitive- perceptive, aware
thrilled-excited, exhilarated
trusting- unguarded, open

#2. Sad
abandoned-rejected, stranded
ashamed- sorry, full of remorse
despair- distressed, miserable, empty
disappointed- upset, crestfallen
depressed - low, upset, unhappy
embarrassed- uneasy, awkward
grief- full of sadness for something lost
guilty- blameworthy, responsible for something bad
hurt- injured (literally or figuratively)
lonely- isolated
vulnerable- unprotected, unsafe
victimized- cheated, tricked

#3. Angry
aggravated- irritated, vexed
annoyed-displeased, exasperated
betrayed-failed, cheated
bitter-resentful of someone else's actions
critical- negative of someone else's actions or your own
disrespected- to be treated rudely/without
disregarded- not considered, distant from loved ones
frustrated- defeated/unable to attain desire
furious- outraged, enraged
hostile- aggressive, warlike
humiliated-embarrassed, shamed
mad- furious
violated-transgressed, disobeyed, defied

Feelings Defined

Also, these are just a few feelings and the definitions aren't all listed. Make sure to jot down the number your feeling falls under. For example, all feelings under happy are #1, so you would note this as #1 in your journal. When you reflect you may notice patterns of feelings and it could help you understand your circumstances better.

#4. Disconnected

apathetic- uninterested
bored- indifferent, detached
busy- overly preoccupied, out-of-control
confused- in a fog, bewildered, perplexed
rushed- hurried
sleepy- sluggish, drowsy
stressed- burdened
tired- fatigued, drained
unfocused- unable to concentrate

#5. Disgusted

awful- very bad or unpleasant
detestable-despicable, obnoxious
disapproving- critical, scathing
disappointed- let down, saddened
embarrassed- awkward, uncomfortable
hesitant- uncertain, doubtful
horrified-terrorized, spooked
judgemental- deciding if others' actions are good/bad
judged- others deciding if your actions are good/bad
nauseated- sickened (literally or figuratively)
numb- unfeeling
revolted- shocked, horrified, repelled

#6. Fearful

anxious- worried, concerned
excluded- left out
exposed- open to criticism or harm, vulnerable
frightened- scared
helpless- weak,vulnerable
inadequate- not good enough
insecure- not feeling safe because of deficiency
nervous-tense, edgy
overwhelmed- to be buried/defeated
persecuted- punished, victimized
rejected- left out because you're inadequate or not good enough
threatened- intimidated
weak- frail, sickly
worried- disturbed, troubled
withdrawn - silent, distant, reserved

Important Vocabulary

Ableism- Discrimination in favor of able-bodied people based on the false belief that an able-bodied person is more valuable than a disabled person; or limiting beliefs about a disabled person. Some examples of unfair ableist treatment: **asking someone what is "wrong" with them** or **saying, "you can't be disabled," as though this is a compliment.** Viewing a person with a disability as inspirational for doing typical things, such as having a career or having meaningful relationships is hurtful to the disabled person because it is not supportive; it implies it is surprising they can do things other humans do regularly.

Accommodation- An arrangement made to help a disabled person thrive in an environment that was not created with their needs in mind. Some examples of accommodations are wheelchair ramps and handicapped parking. Other helpful accommodations might be as simple as warning a sound-sensitive person before turning on a loud appliance like a blender, or encouraging necessary rest breaks when working on a difficult task. It's important to determine what type of accommodations would best help you or your loved one succeed and be safe. Whenever a person is unsure, just ask them what accommodations they need.

Allistic- Any person who is not autistic.

Ally- Someone who joins forces with another to help each other succeed and be safe. When someone needs help, allies believe the person who is asking, then thoughtfully assists the person in need. Allies also never use someone's disability or needs as an insult or a reason to dislike the disabled person.

Autism- A neurological difference compared to neurotypical brains that affects the way people sense the world, think, communicate, and move. Autism is based on a spectrum.

Many people prefer the term "autistic" instead of "having autism" or "person with autism" because it describes one's neurology, which affects every part of life. "Having autism" can make one's neurology sound like an accessory that can be added or taken away when needed, which of course is impossible. If you're unsure how to discuss autism, the best choice is to listen to individuals who are on the spectrum about the language they prefer.

Everyone has some autistic traits because autistic traits are human traits. But we are not all autistic so it would be harmful and wrong to suggest that.

The infinity symbol is the most preferred symbol of autistic people. Rainbow colors are also often used to depict the autism spectrum. Find out more at sensationalstims.com or on Facebook and Instagram @sensationalstims.

Burnout- A state of emotional, physical, and/or mental exhaustion caused by prolonged stress. Burnout prevents a person from accomplishing desired goals and/or necessary tasks. It occurs when a person feels overwhelmed, emotionally drained, and/or unable to meet constant demands. The causes of burnout will vary due to many factors like one's sensory needs, lifestyle, and support system. To prevent burnout, it's important to take time to rest and recharge after doing something demanding.

Disability- Any condition of the body or mind that makes it more difficult for the person with the condition to do certain activities (activity limitation) and interact with the world around them (participation restrictions). Tee Monet, an autistic adult and advocate, notes that autism is a disability because a "disability is anything deviating from what society considers a 'normal' ability. Autism is considered a disability because society commonly functions another way. Disability is not a bad word." To read more of their writings, follow them on Instagram @galaxibrain.

Masking- In this case it means to hide things that might be viewed as socially unacceptable. It's not good to mask because over time it can cause great trauma to the person masking. Asking neurodivergent (ND) people to mask sounds like, "don't move that way because I don't like it." Many neurodivergent people are commonly asked to mask their stims. Requesting someone to mask is an example of ableism. An ally never asks friends to mask.

Meltdown- An intense response to overwhelming circumstances—a complete loss of behavioral control. A meltdown is an involuntary coping mechanism after one's system(s) become(s) overwhelmed with sensory input and/or other stressors. Stimming can help prevent meltdowns.

If you want to be an ally to someone experiencing the distress of a meltdown, give the person privacy, a safe place, and never film him/her/them. Let it pass and don't have them explain the situation as it is happening. Talking may be an option after there's been enough time to rest and recover, if the person is willing and able.

A meltdown is not the same thing as a tantrum and these terms should never be used interchangeably.

Neurology- The way a brain operates/is wired to interpret the world. All people are born with a specific neurology/neurotype which is developed through the person's environment.

Neurotypical (NT)- The neurotype of people who aren't neurodivergent.

Neurodivergent (ND)- The neurotype of people who aren't neurotypical. This term is often used for autistic people, but can also be used for others who aren't autistic, but still neurodivergent. ND refers to unique variation in the way the brain processes information compared to neurotypical processing.

Regulation- Managing sensory and emotional input in a way that helps a person live a happy and healthy life and prevent burnout/meltdowns. Everyone has a unique way to regulate/realign/ ground themselves. There are a variety of ways to regulate one's body, including stimming. Regulation of senses and emotions are required for higher order thinking and executive function. Here are some ways to regulate:

Sit down Rest.
Breathe Put one hand over your heart and one hand over your belly.
Remember You're not in an emergency and slowing down is ok!
Connect Focus on your senses and try to name things you can smell, taste, see, touch, and/or hear.
Count Going backwards or forwards in multiples is a way to refocus your mind.
Honor Acknowledge how you are feeling and that you are an amazing person!

Tantrum- In contrast to a meltdown, is a conscious, voluntary behavior done for the purpose of manipulating another to get a specific reward. Though they might sometimes look similar, knowing the difference between a tantrum and meltdown is crucial to appropriately help people with their unique needs.

Worldview- A way of seeing and understanding the world based on one's unique life experience. People don't all have the same worldview for many reasons and that's ok. Asking people about their needs and experiences is a very positive way to learn, especially about a disability, if you choose to listen and honor the other's worldview.

Other new words I've learned during my wellness journey:

_____

_____

_____

Coloring Page

Coloring Page

Coloring Page

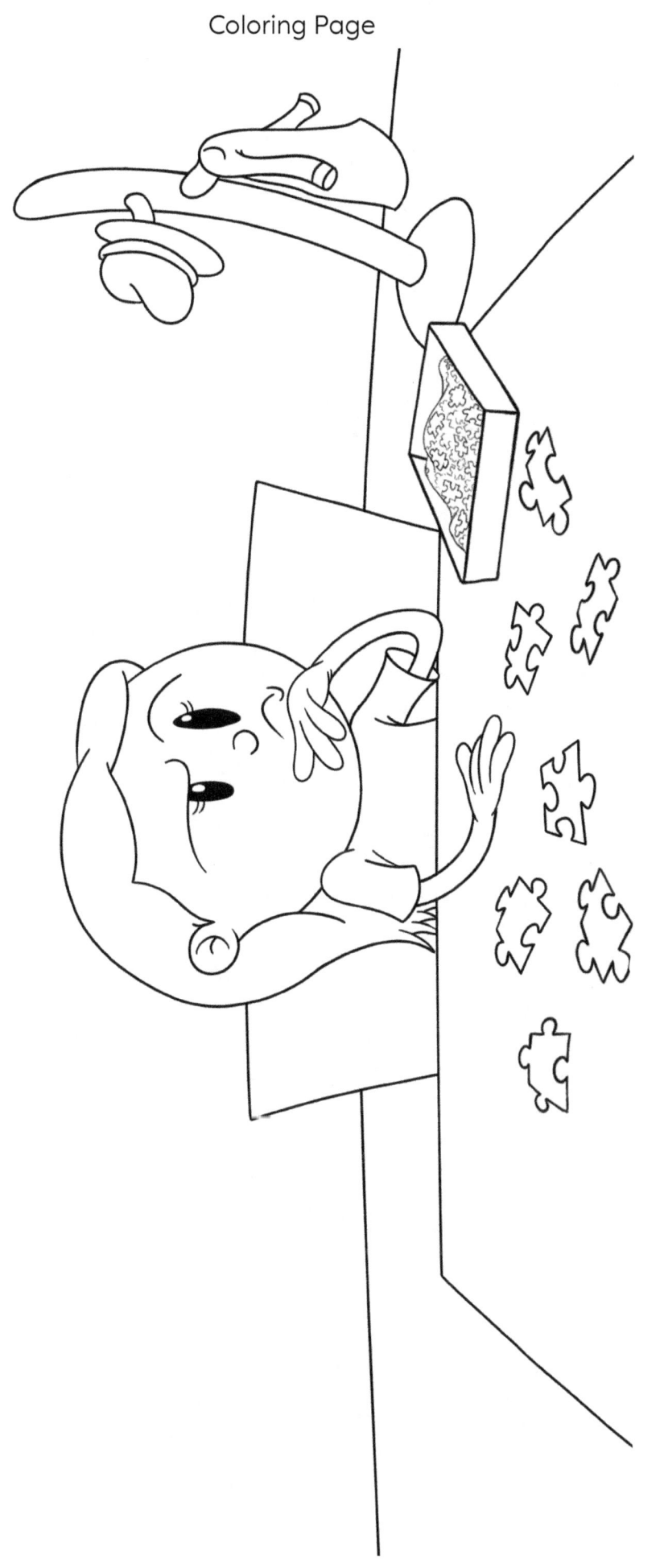

Coloring Page

Doodling Page

Doodling Page

Doodling Page

Doodling Page

Doodling Page

Doodling Page

Doodling Page

Week of:

My positive affirmation for this week is:
(Affirmations are simple, positive statements that everyone can do to frame their mindset. See the next page for definition and help)

As I write this, I am feeling: #_____
(see page 5-6 for feeling words- list what number your feeling falls under. This can help you when you reflect on the feelings you've had over the past few weeks. Any trends? Can you think about why?)

I feel this way because/If I could compare my feelings to something it would be like...

A challenging thing/updates from last week:
(challenges are situations that may have caused you stress. List it here)

I am grateful for/I want to remember:
(The practice of gratitude can change everything in a person's life. Making time to record moments of thankfulness has a powerful impact on your quality of life. Often, gratitude can be an inspirational thing, large or small. What did you notice?)

Have I stimmed lately?
Yes
No

How have I been stimming?

What does my stimming tell me?

Upcoming this week!
(This is to note important upcoming events. They can be related to school, sports, doctors appointments, tv shows- whatever you have coming up!)

Week of :	My positive affirmation for this week is :
	(Affirmations are simple, positive statements that everyone can do to frame their mindset. See the next page for definition and help)

As I write this, I am feeling : #_____
(see page 5-6 for feeling words- list what number your feeling falls under. This can help you when you reflect on the feelings you've had over the past few weeks. Any trends? Can you think about why?)

I feel this way because/If I could compare my feelings to something it would be like...

A challenging thing/updates from last week :
(challenges are situations that may have caused you stress. List it here)

I am grateful for/I want to remember :
(The practice of gratitude can change everything in a person's life. Making time to record moments of thankfulness has a powerful impact on your quality of life. Often, gratitude can be an inspirational thing, large or small. What did you notice?)

Have I stimmed lately?
Yes
No

How have I been stimming?

What does my stimming tell me?

Upcoming this week!
(This is to note important upcoming events. They can be related to school, sports, doctors appointments, tv shows- whatever you have coming up!)

Week of:

My positive affirmation for this week is:
(Affirmations are simple, positive statements that everyone can do to frame their mindset. See the next page for definition and help)

As I write this, I am feeling : #_____
(see page 5-6 for feeling words- list what number your feeling falls under. This can help you when you reflect on the feelings you've had over the past few weeks. Any trends? Can you think about why?)

I feel this way because/If I could compare my feelings to something it would be like...

A challenging thing/updates from last week :
(challenges are situations that may have caused you stress. List it here)

I am grateful for/I want to remember :
(The practice of gratitude can change everything in a person's life. Making time to record moments of thankfulness has a powerful impact on your quality of life. Often, gratitude can be an inspirational thing, large or small. What did you notice?)

Have I stimmed lately?
Yes
No

How have I been stimming?

What does my stimming tell me?

Upcoming this week!
(This is to note important upcoming events. They can be related to school, sports, doctors appointments, tv shows- whatever you have coming up!)

Week of :

My positive affirmation for this week is :
(Affirmations are simple, positive statements that everyone can do to frame their mindset. See the next page for definition and help)

As I write this, I am feeling : #_____
(see page 5-6 for feeling words- list what number your feeling falls under. This can help you when you reflect on the feelings you've had over the past few weeks. Any trends? Can you think about why?)

I feel this way because/If I could compare my feelings to something it would be like...

A challenging thing/updates from last week :
(challenges are situations that may have caused you stress. List it here)

I am grateful for/I want to remember :
(The practice of gratitude can change everything in a person's life. Making time to record moments of thankfulness has a powerful impact on your quality of life. Often, gratitude can be an inspirational thing, large or small. What did you notice?)

Have I stimmed lately?
- Yes
- No

How have I been stimming?

What does my stimming tell me?

Upcoming this week!
(This is to note important upcoming events. They can be related to school, sports, doctors appointments, tv shows- whatever you have coming up!)

Week of :	My positive affirmation for this week is :
	(Affirmations are simple, positive statements that everyone can do to frame their mindset. See the next page for definition and help)

As I write this, I am feeling : #_____
(see page 5-6 for feeling words- list what number your feeling falls under. This can help you when you reflect on the feelings you've had over the past few weeks. Any trends? Can you think about why?)

I feel this way because/If I could compare my feelings to something it would be like...

A challenging thing/updates from last week :
(challenges are situations that may have caused you stress. List it here)

I am grateful for/I want to remember :
(The practice of gratitude can change everything in a person's life. Making time to record moments of thankfulness has a powerful impact on your quality of life. Often, gratitude can be an inspirational thing, large or small. What did you notice?)

Have I stimmed lately? Yes No	How have I been stimming?	What does my stimming tell me?

Upcoming this week!
(This is to note important upcoming events. They can be related to school, sports, doctors appointments, tv shows- whatever you have coming up!)

Week of :

My positive affirmation for this week is :
(Affirmations are simple, positive statements that everyone can do to frame their mindset. See the next page for definition and help)

As I write this, I am feeling : #_____
(see page 5-6 for feeling words- list what number your feeling falls under. This can help you when you reflect on the feelings you've had over the past few weeks. Any trends? Can you think about why?)

I feel this way because/If I could compare my feelings to something it would be like...

A challenging thing/updates from last week :
(challenges are situations that may have caused you stress. List it here)

I am grateful for/I want to remember :
(The practice of gratitude can change everything in a person's life. Making time to record moments of thankfulness has a powerful impact on your quality of life. Often, gratitude can be an inspirational thing, large or small. What did you notice?)

Have I stimmed lately?
　Yes
　No

How have I been stimming?

What does my stimming tell me?

Upcoming this week!
(This is to note important upcoming events. They can be related to school, sports, doctors appointments, tv shows- whatever you have coming up!)

Week of:

My positive affirmation for this week is:
(Affirmations are simple, positive statements that everyone can do to frame their mindset. See the next page for definition and help)

As I write this, I am feeling: #_____
(see page 5-6 for feeling words- list what number your feeling falls under. This can help you when you reflect on the feelings you've had over the past few weeks. Any trends? Can you think about why?)

I feel this way because/If I could compare my feelings to something it would be like...

A challenging thing/updates from last week:
(challenges are situations that may have caused you stress. List it here)

I am grateful for/I want to remember:
(The practice of gratitude can change everything in a person's life. Making time to record moments of thankfulness has a powerful impact on your quality of life. Often, gratitude can be an inspirational thing, large or small. What did you notice?)

Have I stimmed lately?
 Yes
 No

How have I been stimming?

What does my stimming tell me?

Upcoming this week!
(This is to note important upcoming events. They can be related to school, sports, doctors appointments, tv shows- whatever you have coming up!)

Week of :

My positive affirmation for this week is :
(Affirmations are simple, positive statements that everyone can do to frame their mindset. See the next page for definition and help)

As I write this, I am feeling : #_____
(see page 5-6 for feeling words- list what number your feeling falls under. This can help you when you reflect on the feelings you've had over the past few weeks. Any trends? Can you think about why?)

I feel this way because/If I could compare my feelings to something it would be like...

A challenging thing/updates from last week :
(challenges are situations that may have caused you stress. List it here)

I am grateful for/I want to remember :
(The practice of gratitude can change everything in a person's life. Making time to record moments of thankfulness has a powerful impact on your quality of life. Often, gratitude can be an inspirational thing, large or small. What did you notice?)

Have I stimmed lately?
- Yes
- No

How have I been stimming?

What does my stimming tell me?

Upcoming this week!
(This is to note important upcoming events. They can be related to school, sports, doctors appointments, tv shows- whatever you have coming up!)

Week of :	My positive affirmation for this week is :
	(Affirmations are simple, positive statements that everyone can do to frame their mindset. See the next page for definition and help)

As I write this, I am feeling : #_____
(see page 5-6 for feeling words- list what number your feeling falls under. This can help you when you reflect on the feelings you've had over the past few weeks. Any trends? Can you think about why?)

I feel this way because/If I could compare my feelings to something it would be like...

A challenging thing/updates from last week :
(challenges are situations that may have caused you stress. List it here)

I am grateful for/I want to remember :
(The practice of gratitude can change everything in a person's life. Making time to record moments of thankfulness has a powerful impact on your quality of life. Often, gratitude can be an inspirational thing, large or small. What did you notice?)

Have I stimmed lately? Yes No	How have I been stimming?	What does my stimming tell me?

Upcoming this week!
(This is to note important upcoming events. They can be related to school, sports, doctors appointments, tv shows- whatever you have coming up!)

Week of :

My positive affirmation for this week is :
(Affirmations are simple, positive statements that everyone can do to frame their mindset. See the next page for definition and help)

As I write this, I am feeling : #_____
(see page 5-6 for feeling words- list what number your feeling falls under. This can help you when you reflect on the feelings you've had over the past few weeks. Any trends? Can you think about why?)

I feel this way because/If I could compare my feelings to something it would be like...

A challenging thing/updates from last week :
(challenges are situations that may have caused you stress. List it here)

I am grateful for/I want to remember :
(The practice of gratitude can change everything in a person's life. Making time to record moments of thankfulness has a powerful impact on your quality of life. Often, gratitude can be an inspirational thing, large or small. What did you notice?)

Have I stimmed lately?
Yes
No

How have I been stimming?

What does my stimming tell me?

Upcoming this week!
(This is to note important upcoming events. They can be related to school, sports, doctors appointments, tv shows- whatever you have coming up!)

Week of:

My positive affirmation for this week is:
(Affirmations are simple, positive statements that everyone can do to frame their mindset. See the next page for definition and help)

As I write this, I am feeling : #_____
(see page 5-6 for feeling words- list what number your feeling falls under. This can help you when you reflect on the feelings you've had over the past few weeks. Any trends? Can you think about why?)

I feel this way because/If I could compare my feelings to something it would be like...

A challenging thing/updates from last week :
(challenges are situations that may have caused you stress. List it here)

I am grateful for/I want to remember :
(The practice of gratitude can change everything in a person's life. Making time to record moments of thankfulness has a powerful impact on your quality of life. Often, gratitude can be an inspirational thing, large or small. What did you notice?)

Have I stimmed lately?
Yes
No

How have I been stimming?

What does my stimming tell me?

Upcoming this week!
(This is to note important upcoming events. They can be related to school, sports, doctors appointments, tv shows- whatever you have coming up!)

Week of :

My positive affirmation for this week is :
(Affirmations are simple, positive statements that everyone can do to frame their mindset. See the next page for definition and help)

As I write this, I am feeling : #_____
(see page 5-6 for feeling words- list what number your feeling falls under. This can help you when you reflect on the feelings you've had over the past few weeks. Any trends? Can you think about why?)

I feel this way because/If I could compare my feelings to something it would be like...

A challenging thing/updates from last week :
(challenges are situations that may have caused you stress. List it here)

I am grateful for/I want to remember :
(The practice of gratitude can change everything in a person's life. Making time to record moments of thankfulness has a powerful impact on your quality of life. Often, gratitude can be an inspirational thing, large or small. What did you notice?)

Have I stimmed lately?
   Yes
   No

How have I been stimming?

What does my stimming tell me?

Upcoming this week!
(This is to note important upcoming events. They can be related to school, sports, doctors appointments, tv shows- whatever you have coming up!)

Week of :	My positive affirmation for this week is :
	(Affirmations are simple, positive statements that everyone can do to frame their mindset. See the next page for definition and help)

As I write this, I am feeling : #_____
(see page 5-6 for feeling words- list what number your feeling falls under. This can help you when you reflect on the feelings you've had over the past few weeks. Any trends? Can you think about why?)

I feel this way because/If I could compare my feelings to something it would be like...

A challenging thing/updates from last week :
(challenges are situations that may have caused you stress. List it here)

I am grateful for/I want to remember :
(The practice of gratitude can change everything in a person's life. Making time to record moments of thankfulness has a powerful impact on your quality of life. Often, gratitude can be an inspirational thing, large or small. What did you notice?)

Have I stimmed lately? Yes No	How have I been stimming?	What does my stimming tell me?

Upcoming this week!
(This is to note important upcoming events. They can be related to school, sports, doctors appointments, tv shows- whatever you have coming up!)

Week of :

My positive affirmation for this week is :
(Affirmations are simple, positive statements that everyone can do to frame their mindset. See the next page for definition and help)

As I write this, I am feeling : #_____
(see page 5-6 for feeling words- list what number your feeling falls under. This can help you when you reflect on the feelings you've had over the past few weeks. Any trends? Can you think about why?)

I feel this way because/If I could compare my feelings to something it would be like...

A challenging thing/updates from last week :
(challenges are situations that may have caused you stress. List it here)

I am grateful for/I want to remember :
(The practice of gratitude can change everything in a person's life. Making time to record moments of thankfulness has a powerful impact on your quality of life. Often, gratitude can be an inspirational thing, large or small. What did you notice?)

Have I stimmed lately?
  Yes
  No

How have I been stimming?

What does my stimming tell me?

Upcoming this week!
(This is to note important upcoming events. They can be related to school, sports, doctors appointments, tv shows- whatever you have coming up!)

Week of :

My positive affirmation for this week is :
(Affirmations are simple, positive statements that everyone can do to frame their mindset. See the next page for definition and help)

As I write this, I am feeling : #_____
(see page 5-6 for feeling words- list what number your feeling falls under. This can help you when you reflect on the feelings you've had over the past few weeks. Any trends? Can you think about why?)

I feel this way because/If I could compare my feelings to something it would be like...

A challenging thing/updates from last week :
(challenges are situations that may have caused you stress. List it here)

I am grateful for/I want to remember :
(The practice of gratitude can change everything in a person's life. Making time to record moments of thankfulness has a powerful impact on your quality of life. Often, gratitude can be an inspirational thing, large or small. What did you notice?)

Have I stimmed lately?
Yes
No

How have I been stimming?

What does my stimming tell me?

Upcoming this week!
(This is to note important upcoming events. They can be related to school, sports, doctors appointments, tv shows- whatever you have coming up!)

Week of :

My positive affirmation for this week is :
(Affirmations are simple, positive statements that everyone can do to frame their mindset. See the next page for definition and help)

As I write this, I am feeling : #_____
(see page 5-6 for feeling words- list what number your feeling falls under. This can help you when you reflect on the feelings you've had over the past few weeks. Any trends? Can you think about why?)

I feel this way because/If I could compare my feelings to something it would be like...

A challenging thing/updates from last week :
(challenges are situations that may have caused you stress. List it here)

I am grateful for/I want to remember :
(The practice of gratitude can change everything in a person's life. Making time to record moments of thankfulness has a powerful impact on your quality of life. Often, gratitude can be an inspirational thing, large or small. What did you notice?)

Have I stimmed lately?
Yes
No

How have I been stimming?

What does my stimming tell me?

Upcoming this week!
(This is to note important upcoming events. They can be related to school, sports, doctors appointments, tv shows- whatever you have coming up!)

Week of :

My positive affirmation for this week is :
(Affirmations are simple, positive statements that everyone can do to frame their mindset. See the next page for definition and help)

As I write this, I am feeling : #_____
(see page 5-6 for feeling words- list what number your feeling falls under. This can help you when you reflect on the feelings you've had over the past few weeks. Any trends? Can you think about why?)

I feel this way because/If I could compare my feelings to something it would be like...

A challenging thing/updates from last week :
(challenges are situations that may have caused you stress. List it here)

I am grateful for/I want to remember :
(The practice of gratitude can change everything in a person's life. Making time to record moments of thankfulness has a powerful impact on your quality of life. Often, gratitude can be an inspirational thing, large or small. What did you notice?)

Have I stimmed lately?
  Yes
  No

How have I been stimming?

What does my stimming tell me?

Upcoming this week!
(This is to note important upcoming events. They can be related to school, sports, doctors appointments, tv shows- whatever you have coming up!)

Week of :

My positive affirmation for this week is :
(Affirmations are simple, positive statements that everyone can do to frame their mindset. See the next page for definition and help)

As I write this, I am feeling : #_____
(see page 5-6 for feeling words- list what number your feeling falls under. This can help you when you reflect on the feelings you've had over the past few weeks. Any trends? Can you think about why?)

I feel this way because/If I could compare my feelings to something it would be like...

A challenging thing/updates from last week :
(challenges are situations that may have caused you stress. List it here)

I am grateful for/I want to remember :
(The practice of gratitude can change everything in a person's life. Making time to record moments of thankfulness has a powerful impact on your quality of life. Often, gratitude can be an inspirational thing, large or small. What did you notice?)

Have I stimmed lately?
Yes
No

How have I been stimming?

What does my stimming tell me?

Upcoming this week!
(This is to note important upcoming events. They can be related to school, sports, doctors appointments, tv shows- whatever you have coming up!)

Week of :

My positive affirmation for this week is :
(Affirmations are simple, positive statements that everyone can do to frame their mindset. See the next page for definition and help)

As I write this, I am feeling : #_____
(see page 5-6 for feeling words- list what number your feeling falls under. This can help you when you reflect on the feelings you've had over the past few weeks. Any trends? Can you think about why?)

I feel this way because/If I could compare my feelings to something it would be like...

A challenging thing/updates from last week :
(challenges are situations that may have caused you stress. List it here)

I am grateful for/I want to remember :
(The practice of gratitude can change everything in a person's life. Making time to record moments of thankfulness has a powerful impact on your quality of life. Often, gratitude can be an inspirational thing, large or small. What did you notice?)

Have I stimmed lately?
  Yes
  No

How have I been stimming?

What does my stimming tell me?

Upcoming this week!
(This is to note important upcoming events. They can be related to school, sports, doctors appointments, tv shows- whatever you have coming up!)

Week of :

My positive affirmation for this week is :
(Affirmations are simple, positive statements that everyone can do to frame their mindset. See the next page for definition and help)

As I write this, I am feeling : #_____
(see page 5-6 for feeling words- list what number your feeling falls under. This can help you when you reflect on the feelings you've had over the past few weeks. Any trends? Can you think about why?)

I feel this way because/If I could compare my feelings to something it would be like...

A challenging thing/updates from last week :
(challenges are situations that may have caused you stress. List it here)

I am grateful for/I want to remember :
(The practice of gratitude can change everything in a person's life. Making time to record moments of thankfulness has a powerful impact on your quality of life. Often, gratitude can be an inspirational thing, large or small. What did you notice?)

Have I stimmed lately?
Yes
No

How have I been stimming?

What does my stimming tell me?

Upcoming this week!
(This is to note important upcoming events. They can be related to school, sports, doctors appointments, tv shows- whatever you have coming up!)

53

Week of :

My positive affirmation for this week is :
(Affirmations are simple, positive statements that everyone can do to frame their mindset. See the next page for definition and help)

As I write this, I am feeling : #_____
(see page 5-6 for feeling words- list what number your feeling falls under. This can help you when you reflect on the feelings you've had over the past few weeks. Any trends? Can you think about why?)

I feel this way because/If I could compare my feelings to something it would be like...

A challenging thing/updates from last week :
(challenges are situations that may have caused you stress. List it here)

I am grateful for/I want to remember :
(The practice of gratitude can change everything in a person's life. Making time to record moments of thankfulness has a powerful impact on your quality of life. Often, gratitude can be an inspirational thing, large or small. What did you notice?)

Have I stimmed lately?
  Yes
  No

How have I been stimming?

What does my stimming tell me?

Upcoming this week!
(This is to note important upcoming events. They can be related to school, sports, doctors appointments, tv shows- whatever you have coming up!)

Week of :

My positive affirmation for this week is :
(Affirmations are simple, positive statements that everyone can do to frame their mindset. See the next page for definition and help)

As I write this, I am feeling : #_____
(see page 5-6 for feeling words- list what number your feeling falls under. This can help you when you reflect on the feelings you've had over the past few weeks. Any trends? Can you think about why?)

I feel this way because/If I could compare my feelings to something it would be like...

A challenging thing/updates from last week :
(challenges are situations that may have caused you stress. List it here)

I am grateful for/I want to remember :
(The practice of gratitude can change everything in a person's life. Making time to record moments of thankfulness has a powerful impact on your quality of life. Often, gratitude can be an inspirational thing, large or small. What did you notice?)

Have I stimmed lately?
  Yes
  No

How have I been stimming?

What does my stimming tell me?

Upcoming this week!
(This is to note important upcoming events. They can be related to school, sports, doctors appointments, tv shows- whatever you have coming up!)

Week of :	My positive affirmation for this week is :
	(Affirmations are simple, positive statements that everyone can do to frame their mindset. See the next page for definition and help)

As I write this, I am feeling : #_____
(see page 5-6 for feeling words- list what number your feeling falls under. This can help you when you reflect on the feelings you've had over the past few weeks. Any trends? Can you think about why?)

I feel this way because/If I could compare my feelings to something it would be like...

A challenging thing/updates from last week :
(challenges are situations that may have caused you stress. List it here)

I am grateful for/I want to remember :
(The practice of gratitude can change everything in a person's life. Making time to record moments of thankfulness has a powerful impact on your quality of life. Often, gratitude can be an inspirational thing, large or small. What did you notice?)

Have I stimmed lately? Yes No	How have I been stimming?	What does my stimming tell me?

Upcoming this week!
(This is to note important upcoming events. They can be related to school, sports, doctors appointments, tv shows- whatever you have coming up!)

Week of :

My positive affirmation for this week is :
(Affirmations are simple, positive statements that everyone can do to frame their mindset. See the next page for definition and help)

As I write this, I am feeling : #_____
(see page 5-6 for feeling words- list what number your feeling falls under. This can help you when you reflect on the feelings you've had over the past few weeks. Any trends? Can you think about why?)

I feel this way because/If I could compare my feelings to something it would be like...

A challenging thing/updates from last week :
(challenges are situations that may have caused you stress. List it here)

I am grateful for/I want to remember :
(The practice of gratitude can change everything in a person's life. Making time to record moments of thankfulness has a powerful impact on your quality of life. Often, gratitude can be an inspirational thing, large or small. What did you notice?)

Have I stimmed lately?
Yes
No

How have I been stimming?

What does my stimming tell me?

Upcoming this week!
(This is to note important upcoming events. They can be related to school, sports, doctors appointments, tv shows- whatever you have coming up!)

Week of :

My positive affirmation for this week is :
(Affirmations are simple, positive statements that everyone can do to frame their mindset. See the next page for definition and help)

As I write this, I am feeling : #_____
(see page 5-6 for feeling words- list what number your feeling falls under. This can help you when you reflect on the feelings you've had over the past few weeks. Any trends? Can you think about why?)

I feel this way because/If I could compare my feelings to something it would be like...

A challenging thing/updates from last week :
(challenges are situations that may have caused you stress. List it here)

I am grateful for/I want to remember :
(The practice of gratitude can change everything in a person's life. Making time to record moments of thankfulness has a powerful impact on your quality of life. Often, gratitude can be an inspirational thing, large or small. What did you notice?)

Have I stimmed lately?
- Yes
- No

How have I been stimming?

What does my stimming tell me?

Upcoming this week!
(This is to note important upcoming events. They can be related to school, sports, doctors appointments, tv shows- whatever you have coming up!)

Week of :

My positive affirmation for this week is :
(Affirmations are simple, positive statements that everyone can do to frame their mindset. See the next page for definition and help)

As I write this, I am feeling : #_____
(see page 5-6 for feeling words- list what number your feeling falls under. This can help you when you reflect on the feelings you've had over the past few weeks. Any trends? Can you think about why?)

I feel this way because/If I could compare my feelings to something it would be like...

A challenging thing/updates from last week :
(challenges are situations that may have caused you stress. List it here)

I am grateful for/I want to remember :
(The practice of gratitude can change everything in a person's life. Making time to record moments of thankfulness has a powerful impact on your quality of life. Often, gratitude can be an inspirational thing, large or small. What did you notice?)

Have I stimmed lately?
Yes
No

How have I been stimming?

What does my stimming tell me?

Upcoming this week!
(This is to note important upcoming events. They can be related to school, sports, doctors appointments, tv shows- whatever you have coming up!)

Week of :

My positive affirmation for this week is :
(Affirmations are simple, positive statements that everyone can do to frame their mindset. See the next page for definition and help)

As I write this, I am feeling : #_____
(see page 5-6 for feeling words- list what number your feeling falls under. This can help you when you reflect on the feelings you've had over the past few weeks. Any trends? Can you think about why?)

I feel this way because/If I could compare my feelings to something it would be like...

A challenging thing/updates from last week :
(challenges are situations that may have caused you stress. List it here)

I am grateful for/I want to remember :
(The practice of gratitude can change everything in a person's life. Making time to record moments of thankfulness has a powerful impact on your quality of life. Often, gratitude can be an inspirational thing, large or small. What did you notice?)

Have I stimmed lately?
- Yes
- No

How have I been stimming?

What does my stimming tell me?

Upcoming this week!
(This is to note important upcoming events. They can be related to school, sports, doctors appointments, tv shows- whatever you have coming up!)

Week of :

My positive affirmation for this week is :
(Affirmations are simple, positive statements that everyone can do to frame their mindset. See the next page for definition and help)

As I write this, I am feeling : #_____
(see page 5-6 for feeling words- list what number your feeling falls under. This can help you when you reflect on the feelings you've had over the past few weeks. Any trends? Can you think about why?)

I feel this way because/If I could compare my feelings to something it would be like...

A challenging thing/updates from last week :
(challenges are situations that may have caused you stress. List it here)

I am grateful for/I want to remember :
(The practice of gratitude can change everything in a person's life. Making time to record moments of thankfulness has a powerful impact on your quality of life. Often, gratitude can be an inspirational thing, large or small. What did you notice?)

Have I stimmed lately?
   Yes
   No

How have I been stimming?

What does my stimming tell me?

Upcoming this week!
(This is to note important upcoming events. They can be related to school, sports, doctors appointments, tv shows- whatever you have coming up!)

Week of :

My positive affirmation for this week is :
(Affirmations are simple, positive statements that everyone can do to frame their mindset. See the next page for definition and help)

As I write this, I am feeling : #_____
(see page 5-6 for feeling words- list what number your feeling falls under. This can help you when you reflect on the feelings you've had over the past few weeks. Any trends? Can you think about why?)

I feel this way because/If I could compare my feelings to something it would be like...

A challenging thing/updates from last week :
(challenges are situations that may have caused you stress. List it here)

I am grateful for/I want to remember :
(The practice of gratitude can change everything in a person's life. Making time to record moments of thankfulness has a powerful impact on your quality of life. Often, gratitude can be an inspirational thing, large or small. What did you notice?)

Have I stimmed lately?
  Yes
  No

How have I been stimming?

What does my stimming tell me?

Upcoming this week!
(This is to note important upcoming events. They can be related to school, sports, doctors appointments, tv shows- whatever you have coming up!)

Week of :	**My positive affirmation for this week is :**
	(Affirmations are simple, positive statements that everyone can do to frame their mindset. See the next page for definition and help)

As I write this, I am feeling : #_____
(see page 5-6 for feeling words- list what number your feeling falls under. This can help you when you reflect on the feelings you've had over the past few weeks. Any trends? Can you think about why?)

I feel this way because/If I could compare my feelings to something it would be like...

A challenging thing/updates from last week :
(challenges are situations that may have caused you stress. List it here)

I am grateful for/I want to remember :
(The practice of gratitude can change everything in a person's life. Making time to record moments of thankfulness has a powerful impact on your quality of life. Often, gratitude can be an inspirational thing, large or small. What did you notice?)

Have I stimmed lately? Yes No	**How have I been stimming?**	**What does my stimming tell me?**

Upcoming this week!
(This is to note important upcoming events. They can be related to school, sports, doctors appointments, tv shows- whatever you have coming up!)

Week of :

My positive affirmation for this week is :
(Affirmations are simple, positive statements that everyone can do to frame their mindset. See the next page for definition and help)

As I write this, I am feeling : #_____
(see page 5-6 for feeling words- list what number your feeling falls under. This can help you when you reflect on the feelings you've had over the past few weeks. Any trends? Can you think about why?)

I feel this way because/If I could compare my feelings to something it would be like...

A challenging thing/updates from last week :
(challenges are situations that may have caused you stress. List it here)

I am grateful for/I want to remember :
(The practice of gratitude can change everything in a person's life. Making time to record moments of thankfulness has a powerful impact on your quality of life. Often, gratitude can be an inspirational thing, large or small. What did you notice?)

Have I stimmed lately?
  Yes
  No

How have I been stimming?

What does my stimming tell me?

Upcoming this week!
(This is to note important upcoming events. They can be related to school, sports, doctors appointments, tv shows- whatever you have coming up!)

Week of :

My positive affirmation for this week is :
(Affirmations are simple, positive statements that everyone can do to frame their mindset. See the next page for definition and help)

As I write this, I am feeling : #_____
(see page 5-6 for feeling words- list what number your feeling falls under. This can help you when you reflect on the feelings you've had over the past few weeks. Any trends? Can you think about why?)

I feel this way because/If I could compare my feelings to something it would be like...

A challenging thing/updates from last week :
(challenges are situations that may have caused you stress. List it here)

I am grateful for/I want to remember :
(The practice of gratitude can change everything in a person's life. Making time to record moments of thankfulness has a powerful impact on your quality of life. Often, gratitude can be an inspirational thing, large or small. What did you notice?)

Have I stimmed lately?
- Yes
- No

How have I been stimming?

What does my stimming tell me?

Upcoming this week!
(This is to note important upcoming events. They can be related to school, sports, doctors appointments, tv shows- whatever you have coming up!)

Week of :

My positive affirmation for this week is :
(Affirmations are simple, positive statements that everyone can do to frame their mindset. See the next page for definition and help)

As I write this, I am feeling : #_____
(see page 5-6 for feeling words- list what number your feeling falls under. This can help you when you reflect on the feelings you've had over the past few weeks. Any trends? Can you think about why?)

I feel this way because/If I could compare my feelings to something it would be like...

A challenging thing/updates from last week :
(challenges are situations that may have caused you stress. List it here)

I am grateful for/I want to remember :
(The practice of gratitude can change everything in a person's life. Making time to record moments of thankfulness has a powerful impact on your quality of life. Often, gratitude can be an inspirational thing, large or small. What did you notice?)

Have I stimmed lately?
  Yes
  No

How have I been stimming?

What does my stimming tell me?

Upcoming this week!
(This is to note important upcoming events. They can be related to school, sports, doctors appointments, tv shows- whatever you have coming up!)

Week of :

My positive affirmation for this week is :
(Affirmations are simple, positive statements that everyone can do to frame their mindset. See the next page for definition and help)

As I write this, I am feeling : #_____
(see page 5-6 for feeling words- list what number your feeling falls under. This can help you when you reflect on the feelings you've had over the past few weeks. Any trends? Can you think about why?)

I feel this way because/If I could compare my feelings to something it would be like...

A challenging thing/updates from last week :
(challenges are situations that may have caused you stress. List it here)

I am grateful for/I want to remember :
(The practice of gratitude can change everything in a person's life. Making time to record moments of thankfulness has a powerful impact on your quality of life. Often, gratitude can be an inspirational thing, large or small. What did you notice?)

Have I stimmed lately?
- Yes
- No

How have I been stimming?

What does my stimming tell me?

Upcoming this week!
(This is to note important upcoming events. They can be related to school, sports, doctors appointments, tv shows- whatever you have coming up!)

Week of :

My positive affirmation for this week is :
(Affirmations are simple, positive statements that everyone can do to frame their mindset. See the next page for definition and help)

As I write this, I am feeling : #_____
(see page 5-6 for feeling words- list what number your feeling falls under. This can help you when you reflect on the feelings you've had over the past few weeks. Any trends? Can you think about why?)

I feel this way because/If I could compare my feelings to something it would be like...

A challenging thing/updates from last week :
(challenges are situations that may have caused you stress. List it here)

I am grateful for/I want to remember :
(The practice of gratitude can change everything in a person's life. Making time to record moments of thankfulness has a powerful impact on your quality of life. Often, gratitude can be an inspirational thing, large or small. What did you notice?)

Have I stimmed lately?
  Yes
  No

How have I been stimming?

What does my stimming tell me?

Upcoming this week!
(This is to note important upcoming events. They can be related to school, sports, doctors appointments, tv shows- whatever you have coming up!)

Week of :

My positive affirmation for this week is :
(Affirmations are simple, positive statements that everyone can do to frame their mindset. See the next page for definition and help)

As I write this, I am feeling : #_____
(see page 5-6 for feeling words- list what number your feeling falls under. This can help you when you reflect on the feelings you've had over the past few weeks. Any trends? Can you think about why?)

I feel this way because/If I could compare my feelings to something it would be like...

A challenging thing/updates from last week :
(challenges are situations that may have caused you stress. List it here)

I am grateful for/I want to remember :
(The practice of gratitude can change everything in a person's life. Making time to record moments of thankfulness has a powerful impact on your quality of life. Often, gratitude can be an inspirational thing, large or small. What did you notice?)

Have I stimmed lately?
  Yes
  No

How have I been stimming?

What does my stimming tell me?

Upcoming this week!
(This is to note important upcoming events. They can be related to school, sports, doctors appointments, tv shows- whatever you have coming up!)

Week of :

My positive affirmation for this week is :
(Affirmations are simple, positive statements that everyone can do to frame their mindset. See the next page for definition and help)

As I write this, I am feeling : #_____
(see page 5-6 for feeling words- list what number your feeling falls under. This can help you when you reflect on the feelings you've had over the past few weeks. Any trends? Can you think about why?)

I feel this way because/If I could compare my feelings to something it would be like...

A challenging thing/updates from last week :
(challenges are situations that may have caused you stress. List it here)

I am grateful for/I want to remember :
(The practice of gratitude can change everything in a person's life. Making time to record moments of thankfulness has a powerful impact on your quality of life. Often, gratitude can be an inspirational thing, large or small. What did you notice?)

Have I stimmed lately?
Yes
No

How have I been stimming?

What does my stimming tell me?

Upcoming this week!
(This is to note important upcoming events. They can be related to school, sports, doctors appointments, tv shows- whatever you have coming up!)

Week of:

My positive affirmation for this week is:
(Affirmations are simple, positive statements that everyone can do to frame their mindset. See the next page for definition and help)

As I write this, I am feeling : #_____
(see page 5-6 for feeling words- list what number your feeling falls under. This can help you when you reflect on the feelings you've had over the past few weeks. Any trends? Can you think about why?)

I feel this way because/If I could compare my feelings to something it would be like...

A challenging thing/updates from last week:
(challenges are situations that may have caused you stress. List it here)

I am grateful for/I want to remember:
(The practice of gratitude can change everything in a person's life. Making time to record moments of thankfulness has a powerful impact on your quality of life. Often, gratitude can be an inspirational thing, large or small. What did you notice?)

Have I stimmed lately?
- Yes
- No

How have I been stimming?

What does my stimming tell me?

Upcoming this week!
(This is to note important upcoming events. They can be related to school, sports, doctors appointments, tv shows- whatever you have coming up!)

Week of :

My positive affirmation for this week is :
(Affirmations are simple, positive statements that everyone can do to frame their mindset. See the next page for definition and help)

As I write this, I am feeling : #_____
(see page 5-6 for feeling words- list what number your feeling falls under. This can help you when you reflect on the feelings you've had over the past few weeks. Any trends? Can you think about why?)

I feel this way because/If I could compare my feelings to something it would be like...

A challenging thing/updates from last week :
(challenges are situations that may have caused you stress. List it here)

I am grateful for/I want to remember :
(The practice of gratitude can change everything in a person's life. Making time to record moments of thankfulness has a powerful impact on your quality of life. Often, gratitude can be an inspirational thing, large or small. What did you notice?)

Have I stimmed lately?
- Yes
- No

How have I been stimming?

What does my stimming tell me?

Upcoming this week!
(This is to note important upcoming events. They can be related to school, sports, doctors appointments, tv shows- whatever you have coming up!)

Week of :

My positive affirmation for this week is :
(Affirmations are simple, positive statements that everyone can do to frame their mindset. See the next page for definition and help)

As I write this, I am feeling : #_____
(see page 5-6 for feeling words- list what number your feeling falls under. This can help you when you reflect on the feelings you've had over the past few weeks. Any trends? Can you think about why?)

I feel this way because/If I could compare my feelings to something it would be like...

A challenging thing/updates from last week :
(challenges are situations that may have caused you stress. List it here)

I am grateful for/I want to remember :
(The practice of gratitude can change everything in a person's life. Making time to record moments of thankfulness has a powerful impact on your quality of life. Often, gratitude can be an inspirational thing, large or small. What did you notice?)

Have I stimmed lately?
- Yes
- No

How have I been stimming?

What does my stimming tell me?

Upcoming this week!
(This is to note important upcoming events. They can be related to school, sports, doctors appointments, tv shows- whatever you have coming up!)

Week of :

My positive affirmation for this week is :
(Affirmations are simple, positive statements that everyone can do to frame their mindset. See the next page for definition and help)

As I write this, I am feeling : #_____
(see page 5-6 for feeling words- list what number your feeling falls under. This can help you when you reflect on the feelings you've had over the past few weeks. Any trends? Can you think about why?)

I feel this way because/If I could compare my feelings to something it would be like...

A challenging thing/updates from last week :
(challenges are situations that may have caused you stress. List it here)

I am grateful for/I want to remember :
(The practice of gratitude can change everything in a person's life. Making time to record moments of thankfulness has a powerful impact on your quality of life. Often, gratitude can be an inspirational thing, large or small. What did you notice?)

Have I stimmed lately?
  Yes
  No

How have I been stimming?

What does my stimming tell me?

Upcoming this week!
(This is to note important upcoming events. They can be related to school, sports, doctors appointments, tv shows- whatever you have coming up!)

Week of :

My positive affirmation for this week is :
(Affirmations are simple, positive statements that everyone can do to frame their mindset. See the next page for definition and help)

As I write this, I am feeling : #_____
(see page 5-6 for feeling words- list what number your feeling falls under. This can help you when you reflect on the feelings you've had over the past few weeks. Any trends? Can you think about why?)

I feel this way because/If I could compare my feelings to something it would be like...

A challenging thing/updates from last week :
(challenges are situations that may have caused you stress. List it here)

I am grateful for/I want to remember :
(The practice of gratitude can change everything in a person's life. Making time to record moments of thankfulness has a powerful impact on your quality of life. Often, gratitude can be an inspirational thing, large or small. What did you notice?)

Have I stimmed lately?
- Yes
- No

How have I been stimming?

What does my stimming tell me?

Upcoming this week!
(This is to note important upcoming events. They can be related to school, sports, doctors appointments, tv shows- whatever you have coming up!)

Week of :

My positive affirmation for this week is :
(Affirmations are simple, positive statements that everyone can do to frame their mindset. See the next page for definition and help)

As I write this, I am feeling : #_____
(see page 5-6 for feeling words- list what number your feeling falls under. This can help you when you reflect on the feelings you've had over the past few weeks. Any trends? Can you think about why?)

I feel this way because/If I could compare my feelings to something it would be like...

A challenging thing/updates from last week :
(challenges are situations that may have caused you stress. List it here)

I am grateful for/I want to remember :
(The practice of gratitude can change everything in a person's life. Making time to record moments of thankfulness has a powerful impact on your quality of life. Often, gratitude can be an inspirational thing, large or small. What did you notice?)

Have I stimmed lately?
Yes
No

How have I been stimming?

What does my stimming tell me?

Upcoming this week!
(This is to note important upcoming events. They can be related to school, sports, doctors appointments, tv shows- whatever you have coming up!)

Week of :

My positive affirmation for this week is :
(Affirmations are simple, positive statements that everyone can do to frame their mindset. See the next page for definition and help)

As I write this, I am feeling : #_____
(see page 5-6 for feeling words- list what number your feeling falls under. This can help you when you reflect on the feelings you've had over the past few weeks. Any trends? Can you think about why?)

I feel this way because/If I could compare my feelings to something it would be like...

A challenging thing/updates from last week :
(challenges are situations that may have caused you stress. List it here)

I am grateful for/I want to remember :
(The practice of gratitude can change everything in a person's life. Making time to record moments of thankfulness has a powerful impact on your quality of life. Often, gratitude can be an inspirational thing, large or small. What did you notice?)

Have I stimmed lately?
- Yes
- No

How have I been stimming?

What does my stimming tell me?

Upcoming this week!
(This is to note important upcoming events. They can be related to school, sports, doctors appointments, tv shows- whatever you have coming up!)

Week of :

My positive affirmation for this week is :
(Affirmations are simple, positive statements that everyone can do to frame their mindset. See the next page for definition and help)

As I write this, I am feeling : #_____
(see page 5-6 for feeling words- list what number your feeling falls under. This can help you when you reflect on the feelings you've had over the past few weeks. Any trends? Can you think about why?)

I feel this way because/If I could compare my feelings to something it would be like...

A challenging thing/updates from last week :
(challenges are situations that may have caused you stress. List it here)

I am grateful for/I want to remember :
(The practice of gratitude can change everything in a person's life. Making time to record moments of thankfulness has a powerful impact on your quality of life. Often, gratitude can be an inspirational thing, large or small. What did you notice?)

Have I stimmed lately?
  Yes
  No

How have I been stimming?

What does my stimming tell me?

Upcoming this week!
(This is to note important upcoming events. They can be related to school, sports, doctors appointments, tv shows- whatever you have coming up!)

Week of :

My positive affirmation for this week is :
(Affirmations are simple, positive statements that everyone can do to frame their mindset. See the next page for definition and help)

As I write this, I am feeling : #_____
(see page 5-6 for feeling words- list what number your feeling falls under. This can help you when you reflect on the feelings you've had over the past few weeks. Any trends? Can you think about why?)

I feel this way because/If I could compare my feelings to something it would be like...

A challenging thing/updates from last week :
(challenges are situations that may have caused you stress. List it here)

I am grateful for/I want to remember :
(The practice of gratitude can change everything in a person's life. Making time to record moments of thankfulness has a powerful impact on your quality of life. Often, gratitude can be an inspirational thing, large or small. What did you notice?)

Have I stimmed lately?
- Yes
- No

How have I been stimming?

What does my stimming tell me?

Upcoming this week!
(This is to note important upcoming events. They can be related to school, sports, doctors appointments, tv shows- whatever you have coming up!)

Week of:

My positive affirmation for this week is:
(Affirmations are simple, positive statements that everyone can do to frame their mindset. See the next page for definition and help)

As I write this, I am feeling: #_____
(see page 5-6 for feeling words- list what number your feeling falls under. This can help you when you reflect on the feelings you've had over the past few weeks. Any trends? Can you think about why?)

I feel this way because/If I could compare my feelings to something it would be like...

A challenging thing/updates from last week:
(challenges are situations that may have caused you stress. List it here)

I am grateful for/I want to remember:
(The practice of gratitude can change everything in a person's life. Making time to record moments of thankfulness has a powerful impact on your quality of life. Often, gratitude can be an inspirational thing, large or small. What did you notice?)

Have I stimmed lately?
- Yes
- No

How have I been stimming?

What does my stimming tell me?

Upcoming this week!
(This is to note important upcoming events. They can be related to school, sports, doctors appointments, tv shows- whatever you have coming up!)

Week of :

My positive affirmation for this week is :
(Affirmations are simple, positive statements that everyone can do to frame their mindset. See the next page for definition and help)

As I write this, I am feeling : #_____
(see page 5-6 for feeling words- list what number your feeling falls under. This can help you when you reflect on the feelings you've had over the past few weeks. Any trends? Can you think about why?)

I feel this way because/If I could compare my feelings to something it would be like...

A challenging thing/updates from last week :
(challenges are situations that may have caused you stress. List it here)

I am grateful for/I want to remember :
(The practice of gratitude can change everything in a person's life. Making time to record moments of thankfulness has a powerful impact on your quality of life. Often, gratitude can be an inspirational thing, large or small. What did you notice?)

Have I stimmed lately?
  Yes
  No

How have I been stimming?

What does my stimming tell me?

Upcoming this week!
(This is to note important upcoming events. They can be related to school, sports, doctors appointments, tv shows- whatever you have coming up!)

Week of :

My positive affirmation for this week is :
(Affirmations are simple, positive statements that everyone can do to frame their mindset. See the next page for definition and help)

As I write this, I am feeling : #_____
(see page 5-6 for feeling words- list what number your feeling falls under. This can help you when you reflect on the feelings you've had over the past few weeks. Any trends? Can you think about why?)

I feel this way because/If I could compare my feelings to something it would be like...

A challenging thing/updates from last week :
(challenges are situations that may have caused you stress. List it here)

I am grateful for/I want to remember :
(The practice of gratitude can change everything in a person's life. Making time to record moments of thankfulness has a powerful impact on your quality of life. Often, gratitude can be an inspirational thing, large or small. What did you notice?)

Have I stimmed lately?
  Yes
  No

How have I been stimming?

What does my stimming tell me?

Upcoming this week!
(This is to note important upcoming events. They can be related to school, sports, doctors appointments, tv shows- whatever you have coming up!)

Week of :

My positive affirmation for this week is :
(Affirmations are simple, positive statements that everyone can do to frame their mindset. See the next page for definition and help)

As I write this, I am feeling : #_____
(see page 5-6 for feeling words- list what number your feeling falls under. This can help you when you reflect on the feelings you've had over the past few weeks. Any trends? Can you think about why?)

I feel this way because/If I could compare my feelings to something it would be like...

A challenging thing/updates from last week :
(challenges are situations that may have caused you stress. List it here)

I am grateful for/I want to remember :
(The practice of gratitude can change everything in a person's life. Making time to record moments of thankfulness has a powerful impact on your quality of life. Often, gratitude can be an inspirational thing, large or small. What did you notice?)

Have I stimmed lately?
  Yes
  No

How have I been stimming?

What does my stimming tell me?

Upcoming this week!
(This is to note important upcoming events. They can be related to school, sports, doctors appointments, tv shows- whatever you have coming up!)

Week of :

My positive affirmation for this week is :
(Affirmations are simple, positive statements that everyone can do to frame their mindset. See the next page for definition and help)

As I write this, I am feeling : #_____
(see page 5-6 for feeling words- list what number your feeling falls under. This can help you when you reflect on the feelings you've had over the past few weeks. Any trends? Can you think about why?)

I feel this way because/If I could compare my feelings to something it would be like...

A challenging thing/updates from last week :
(challenges are situations that may have caused you stress. List it here)

I am grateful for/I want to remember :
(The practice of gratitude can change everything in a person's life. Making time to record moments of thankfulness has a powerful impact on your quality of life. Often, gratitude can be an inspirational thing, large or small. What did you notice?)

Have I stimmed lately?
- Yes
- No

How have I been stimming?

What does my stimming tell me?

Upcoming this week!
(This is to note important upcoming events. They can be related to school, sports, doctors appointments, tv shows- whatever you have coming up!)

Week of :

My positive affirmation for this week is :
(Affirmations are simple, positive statements that everyone can do to frame their mindset. See the next page for definition and help)

As I write this, I am feeling : #_____
(see page 5-6 for feeling words- list what number your feeling falls under. This can help you when you reflect on the feelings you've had over the past few weeks. Any trends? Can you think about why?)

A challenging thing/updates from last week :
(challenges are situations that may have caused you stress. List it here)

I feel this way because/If I could compare my feelings to something it would be like...

I am grateful for/I want to remember :
(The practice of gratitude can change everything in a person's life. Making time to record moments of thankfulness has a powerful impact on your quality of life. Often, gratitude can be an inspirational thing, large or small. What did you notice?)

Have I stimmed lately?
   Yes
   No

How have I been stimming?

What does my stimming tell me?

Upcoming this week!
(This is to note important upcoming events. They can be related to school, sports, doctors appointments, tv shows- whatever you have coming up!)

Week of :

My positive affirmation for this week is :
(Affirmations are simple, positive statements that everyone can do to frame their mindset. See the next page for definition and help)

As I write this, I am feeling : #_____
(see page 5-6 for feeling words- list what number your feeling falls under. This can help you when you reflect on the feelings you've had over the past few weeks. Any trends? Can you think about why?)

I feel this way because/If I could compare my feelings to something it would be like...

A challenging thing/updates from last week :
(challenges are situations that may have caused you stress. List it here)

I am grateful for/I want to remember :
(The practice of gratitude can change everything in a person's life. Making time to record moments of thankfulness has a powerful impact on your quality of life. Often, gratitude can be an inspirational thing, large or small. What did you notice?)

Have I stimmed lately?
  Yes
  No

How have I been stimming?

What does my stimming tell me?

Upcoming this week!
(This is to note important upcoming events. They can be related to school, sports, doctors appointments, tv shows- whatever you have coming up!)

Week of :

My positive affirmation for this week is :
(Affirmations are simple, positive statements that everyone can do to frame their mindset. See the next page for definition and help)

As I write this, I am feeling : #_____
(see page 5-6 for feeling words- list what number your feeling falls under. This can help you when you reflect on the feelings you've had over the past few weeks. Any trends? Can you think about why?)

I feel this way because/If I could compare my feelings to something it would be like...

A challenging thing/updates from last week :
(challenges are situations that may have caused you stress. List it here)

I am grateful for/I want to remember :
(The practice of gratitude can change everything in a person's life. Making time to record moments of thankfulness has a powerful impact on your quality of life. Often, gratitude can be an inspirational thing, large or small. What did you notice?)

Have I stimmed lately?
  Yes
  No

How have I been stimming?

What does my stimming tell me?

Upcoming this week!
(This is to note important upcoming events. They can be related to school, sports, doctors appointments, tv shows- whatever you have coming up!)

Notes

Notes

Notes

Notes

Notes

Notes

Notes

Notes

Notes

Notes

Your Year in Review

It's the end of one year and the beginning of the next! A brand new year can bring about different feelings for everyone: sometimes happy, sometimes sad. But for right now, it's a good idea to reflect on what you've done, what you've thought, and what you've felt. If you have consistently made entries in this journal, it will be easy to notice how rich with experience your life is! And if you haven't made weekly entries? No problem. You can start today! Take some time to flip through this journal and remember the little things. See how brave and brilliant you are! We hope you have a wonderful year and don't forget to order next year's journal!

Here are some questions to ponder. Choose as many as you'd like to answer or feel free to utilize the "notes" at the end if you want to reflect in your own way.

1. What is an important lesson I learned this year?

_____

_____

_____

2. What is something you accomplished this year that you are proud of?

_____

_____

_____

3. What was the nicest thing someone did for you this year?

_____

_____

_____

4. What was the nicest thing you did for someone else this year?

_____

_____

_____

5. List 10 things you are grateful for.

_____

_____

_____

6. What did you change your mind about this year?

_____

_____

_____

7. What was one of the funniest things that happened this year?

_____

_____

_____

8. What was one of your most challenging experiences this year?

_____

_____

_____

9. If you could describe this year in one word, what would it be and why?

_____

_____

_____

10. What is one word you want to describe next year? Why?

_____

_____

_____

11. (Re)discovering your senses" on page ___. Has anything changed? Note them on that page!

_____

_____

_____

About the Authors and Designer

Erin Garcia is a neurodivergent public educator and writer in California where she lives with her husband, 8 and 9 year old kids, and two poodles. Her maiden name is Dieterle (Dee-ter-lee) which roughly translates from German to "little warrior of the people". She co-authored Tiger Livy and founded Infinite Inclusion Inc., a nonprofit dedicated to making life more inclusive through art. Erin's mission is to create enthusiastic allies who cultivate empathy in their communities. The Case of Sensational Stims and The Sensational Journal! were inspired by her desire to make the world better. Learn more about what else Erin is up to at eringarciabooks.com or sensationalstims.com

Christian Bajusz (pronounced Bay-ihs) is an artist on the autism spectrum who lives in Virginia. His last name means "mustache" in Hungarian. When he was seven, he taught himself how to draw by studying classic cartoons like Mickey Mouse and Popeye, and has been working hard ever since. He dreams of having his own cartoon series one day. When he's not drawing, Christian enjoys researching and creating archives of old TV broadcasts. If you want to see his latest work, find him on Twitter @CDCBsVCR.

Ashlyn Dickerson is a graphic designer who specializes in digital illustration, page layout, and marketing, but also enjoys fine arts such as ceramics and painting. When she's not honing her art or doting on Akira, her beautiful lab-mix rescue pup, you can find her hanging out with her husband, friends, watching Netflix, eating spicy food, or listening to hardcore metal music. She values mental, emotional, and physical health immensely. Check out her latest projects at www.bluupnda.com.

Join the @sensationalstims community where we talk about stimming, autism, and all kinds of sensational things! We are on Instagram, Facebook, or sensationalstims.com (with parent permission, of course).

www.ingramcontent.com/pod-product-compliance
Lightning Source LLC
Chambersburg PA
CBHW081710100526
44590CB00022B/3726